The Maori
in colour

ISBN 0-908563-77-9

A Microtone® Colour Book
text by Don Sinclair

The publishers acknowledge the assistance of the Department of Maori Affairs

The Caxton Press, Christchurch

HE IWI TAHI TATOU

Where should we begin this little book on the Maori people? Where more fitting than at Waitangi in the far north of New Zealand: it was here on the 6th of February 1840, during the signing of the Treaty of Waitangi, that these words were spoken. "He iwi tāhi tātou – we are one people." All New Zealanders are reminded of this on their annual holiday which commemorates that historic occasion.

Each year the Treaty anniversary is marked by a ceremony notable for the colourful Maori ceremonial which attends it. The impressive setting in the grounds of the historic Treaty House adds traditional dignity to the celebration. Here on the *marae* (meeting place), close to a superbly carved *whare runanga* (meeting house), the Maori welcoming party assembles to perform the *wero* (challenge), the *powhiri* (action song of welcome), and to provide the *kinaki* (relish – complement) for the speeches. One of the most important of these orations is given by a Maori "elder statesman" – a man held in great regard and noted for his deep knowledge of Maori lore and history.

When the formal ceremony is finished the Maori party continues to entertain the spectators with action songs and dances, while the crowd slowly disperses. So, it is at a *marae* and meeting house such as those at Waitangi, that in the well practised activities of the people, Maori culture is preserved, customs hallowed by the years are kept alive, and there is a constant renewing of interest in this, our great national heritage.

It is a characteristic of the Maori race that no important undertaking proceeds without due regard to age-old traditions. The construction of this interesting carved house and its attendant war canoe, was no exception. Before the trees used in the timbers were felled, *karakia* (incantations), were chanted to placate *Tane-manuta,* the god of the forest, and the builders worked under strict *tapu* (ceremonial restrictions).

The opening of the house, performed at daybreak by a *tohunga* (priest or wise man), and a high ranking woman, was a solemn occasion calling for a precise ritual which is employed whenever a new *whare runanga* is ready for use. An ancient incantation sends back to *Tane-mahuta* his forest sprites which inhabit the wood used in the building, then crossing the threshold the woman lifts the *tapu* – the house is now freed from the restrictions which up to that time had allowed only those working on it and who were specially protected, to enter.

There are many such carved houses in New Zealand, each one revered by the tribe on whose *marae* it stands, for in it their tribal origins and history are embodied. It is a place with great *mana* (prestige and power), and is cherished and respected, for it is the focal point of all important tribal affairs and activities.

This house at Waitangi is unique in that the interior *poupou* (slab carvings), symbolise the traditions of a number of tribes. Usually it is only the tribe on whose *marae* the house stands, which is featured in the interior carvings. But this house is a national cultural centre, rather than a tribal meeting house.

At Waitangi during the ceremony held annually to commemorate the signing of the Treaty. ABOVE: *The* wero *(challenge) to the Governor-General, as the official party approaches the* marae. BELOW: *The Maori welcoming party rests as the Naval Guard of Honour is inspected.*

HOW HAS MAORI CULTURE SURVIVED?

Only about eight per cent of the New Zealand population is Maori. How then has the language and culture survived? There was no system of hieroglyphics or written script. Wood – a fragile substance in archaeological terms – was the principal material on which the heroes of tribal mythology and folk lore were depicted. The records of the race were oral, and it is remarkable that even today there are a few *kaumātua* (learned elders), who can recite the complicated genealogies, chant the history and tell the ancient tales which have been handed down by word of mouth through the generations. Over the past century, through the dedicated efforts of scholars of both races, Maori and *Pākehā* (white men) alike, much has been recorded and published, and research still continues. But that is only part of the reason.

The answer probably lies in the sentiment expressed in our opening paragraph – "We are now one people." Today, outnumbered the Maori may be; his old life style discarded, his social order integrated with the Pakeha – but overwhelmed he is not. Unrestricted by any legal limitations, he is a citizen who plays a full part in the affairs of contemporary society yet remains a Maori proud of his origins.

The traditional Maori hongi *(greeting). Hands are clasped and noses lightly touched together.*

A group of kuia *(respected elderly women), who with vibrant chanting and beckoning greenery, welcome visitors onto the* marae. *The green leaves worn on the heads indicate that the occasion is a* tangi *(a time of mourning for the dead).*

With this equality, and engendered by it goes a mutual respect. This is a tribute to the fine hereditary characteristics of the race as a whole, and to the integrity and energy of its leaders. It is a monument too to some of the early British legislators, through whose wisdom laws were framed to deter those who sought to exploit the resident Maoris, whose lands they had invaded.

Those early days of European settlement brought sadness and distress to the Maori people, but their own strong social order did much to hold the race together, and to keep them aloof from economic domination. Disorietation, even in the darkest days, did not lure them into becoming a source of cheap labour. Work they did, and do, but on even terms with all other New Zealanders.

During the 1840s many of the tribal chieftains were quick to recognise the benefits, social and material, which came with the colonists, and extended the hand of friendship to them. But as the incoming tide of settlers flowed faster, a feverish and unstable period followed. Distrust and antagonism grew on both sides. These same leaders were then equally quick to go to war in defence of the rights of their people; rights which were in the stress of the times violated, sometimes wilfully, more often thoughtlessly, and frequently unwittingly, by the newly arrived colonists. From this trial of strength the Maori emerged undefeated and with an enhanced reputation. In the negotiations which followed his reasoned eloquence in debate won him many favourable legal decisions. The basis for active Maori participation in the government of the country was laid during this time.

Since then successive Maori leaders, some of them occupying the highest posts in national and local government, have worked untiringly for the welfare of their people. The results of their stewardship are everywhere evident today, for the lives of all New Zealanders – and indeed of the visitors to this country – are enriched by their contact with the Maori people and their distinctive culture.

In New Zealand since earliest times there has always been a great deal of inter-marriage throughout the whole of the social scale; with each succeeding generation the numbers increase. So, Maori blood relationships play a significant role in the nation's pride in, and in the vitality of, *Maoritanga* (Maori culture).

The Maori then, has faced the changing pattern of his life style in a spirit perhaps best expressed in the message that loved Maori leader and scholar, the late Sir Apirana Ngata, wrote in the autograph book of a young girl. Translated by the late Canon Hohepa Taepa, it reads:

"Grow up o tender plant, to fulfil the needs of your generation, your hand to the technical skills and professions of the Pakeha, as a means for your advancement; your heart centred on your Maori culture for your inspiration. Wear it, a plume upon your head; and your soul dedicated to God, the author of all things."

St Mary's Church at Tikitiki on the East Coast; the interior is rich in examples of the best of Maori art and craftsmanship. Sir Apirana Ngata who lived nearby, led the renaissance of Maori culture. Services in this and many other churches are conducted in Maori.

MAORI LANGUAGE STILL LIVES

The mother tongue of the Maori is soft and fluid. There are no harsh guttural sounds, no two consonants come together and each syllable and every word ends with a vowel. The sound of the spoken word is not unlike Italian in its musical cadences.

There are fifteen sounds in all, the five vowels (a, e, i, o, u), and ten consonants (h, k, n, ng, p, r, t, w, and wh). To learn correct pronounciation is relatively simple, but all the vowels have long and short sounds and any mistake may dramatically alter the sense of a word or sentence. The five short-sound vowels are sounded as follows, a as u in *cut*, e as e in men, i as i in kit, o as o in port, u as u in *put*. The long-sound vowels are a as a in father, e as ai in p*ai*r, i as ee in meet, o as o in lore, u as oo in boot. The consonants h, k, m, n, p, r, t and w are sounded as in English, but *ng* has the sound of the last two letters in the word bring, and *wh* is sounded as an aspirated f.

In this book long vowel sounds in Maori words are indicated with a macron.

The Maori vocabulary is extensive and is notable for its abstract concepts, some of which may be readily demonstrated by translating certain well known New Zealand place names, e.g. *Te Mata* – the name of an impressive geographical feature in Hawke's Bay, whose 400m peak is an unrivalled look-out spot from which to view countryside. The derivation of the name is now uncertain, but it can be translated several ways:

Mātā – a heap; referring to its heaped up appearance.
Mata – a face; viewed from afar the skyline has a facelike outline.
Matā – a flint knife.

The first two possibilities are clearly based on tangible factors, but the third, which may be the original and correct meaning, could refer to an historical incident when the survivors from a raid on a nearby *pa* (fortified village), fled to the peak, and in the customary rite of mourning for their kinsfolk, lacerated themselves with cutting flints.

In the same district, Hawke's Bay, is the celebrated place name of 57 letters, *Taumatawhakatangihangakoauauotamateapokaiwhenuakitanatahu.* The translation of this, the longest of all New Zealand place names is given on the Automobile Association signpost which marks the location as "The brow of the hill where Tamatea who travelled all over the land played the flute to his lover."

The missionary William Yate, who in the 1820s worked in New Zealand translating the Bible and other religious writings into Maori, commented on the richness of the language in his book, *An Account of New Zealand:*

"It abounds with words, and with varieties of expression . . . It will scarcely be credited, when stated, that the New Zealanders have a distinct name for every tree and plant in their land; of which there are six or seven hundred, or more different kinds. . . . It is so likewise with respect to birds, fishes, insects, garments, and everything else they possess: and I have never found a native at a loss to express any of the passions, feelings, sensations; any thing connected with joy, sorrow, good, evil; or any qualities of matter, as broad, long, sharp, obtuse, fluid, solid etc. In short, there is scarcely any thing which we can imagine, but they have an expression for it . . . "

Since purely Maori communities have now almost vanished from New Zealand the modern Maori is bi-lingual, or partly so. Those who do not now speak their own language fluently can usually understand it. It is good to be able to record that after many years of neglect, there is today active encouragement in universities, teacher's training colleges and secondary and primary schools for the teaching and learning of the language. The now flourishing interest is shared by Maori and Pakeha, for the Maori language is now recognised as a precious national asset.

For those who are studying the Maori language – and each year sees an increasing number of people doing so – there are now many excellent textbooks, dictionaries, and sound recordings available. *Te Ao Hou,* a magazine published by the Maori Affairs Department, has done much to stimulate the written use of the language, and to encourage contemporary literary expression, especially among the younger Maori writers.

Allegories, personification and imagery are characteristic features of Maori speech, and though to the old-time Maori rhyme was unknown, rhythm played a vital part not only in his speech but also in his daily living. His ancient chants and songs, his formal greetings and modes of address, take on a recitative form and are often accompanied by gestures which add emphasis to the spoken word.

When Maori people meet together for a *hui* (formal gathering), as they often do, the role of the orator is paramount. Speeches are the order of the day, and it is not sufficient that the orator be a fluent speaker, he must also possess a detailed knowledge of etiquette and be word perfect in the historical allusions, proverbs and tribal lore which is woven into every address, no matter the subject.

Chants too, are often interpolated throughout a speech. These are of great moment to the audience, and though they may sound tuneless to the untrained ear, they are euphonious and are recited in a quite remarkable fashion. Long passages are chanted without pausing for breath, and on occasion more than one voice is employed to ensure that there will be no break in the rendering. This uninterrupted delivery is reckoned to be very important in the case of an incantation; a pause would destroy the efficacy. A speech may also incorporate, and usually ends with a song, the speaker's supporters among the listeners spontaneously joining in with restraint or with vigour, according to the sentiment. This could be concerned with almost any subject from a lament to a lullaby, a taunt, to a song of friendship, or even a ballad in honour of a distinguished visitor.

It is on these occasions on the *marae,* that the Maori language is seen to be still a living and vital force in the land. Over the years, many an elder has concluded his speech with the plea: *"Kia ū ki tō tātou Māoritanga, me ngā mahi a ngā tūpuna* – Let us hold fast to our Maoritanga, and to the ways of our forbears"*.

Whaikōrero *(an oration). Gifted and scholarly* kaumātua *(elders), many of them warriors – as were their forefathers – keep the Maori language alive and vital. These men take pride in their detailed knowledge of their tribal histories.*

MAORI ACTION SONGS OF YESTERDAY AND TODAY

Most people are familiar with the vigorous posture dance performed by New Zealand sporting teams before the start of an international match. This spectacular item is always a stirring preliminary, but few spectators realise its origins. Popularly called a Maori war dance, it is perhaps more properly a *haka pūkana*. *Haka* is the generic term for many different dances which are

With a brandishing of the taiaha *(wooden weapon), the* wero *ends and the women begin the* pōwhiri *(action song of welcome), in front of the carved house "Te Paku-o-te-Rangi" at Putiki Pa, Wanganui.*

The colourful costuming of the modern Maori concert party can be seen in detail in the dress worn by these men and women as they perform an action song.

accompanied by songs with actions. In contrast to the *pūkana* (grimacing) haka, with its shouted, menacing chorus, rolling eyes, protruding tongues and stamping feet is the *poi* dance, performed gracefully by women to a gentle but spirited vocal refrain timed with the twirling of the *poi*, (traditionally a small flax ball stuffed with the down of the *raupo* (bulrush) flower, but now usually made of more modern materials). The *poi* are attached to a thong and in perfect rhythm spin, twirl and tap to accompany the supple movements of the dancers.

These examples are but two of many traditional Maori action songs. All such songs are a pantomime, the body movements and facial expressions being part of the subject of the dance. *Haka* and their vocal *waiata* (songs), are composed and performed to mark an occasion. This may be one of joy, of sadness, of welcome, of farewell, of protest, or perhaps of gratitude – in fact a haka or a waiata may commemorate any incident, historical or contemporary, of moment to the performers and their audience. The Maori loves to sing, has a fine voice and a wonderful natural ability to harmonise; consequently many Maori action songs today are a blend of both cultures. European style melodies and musical instruments have been adopted, but Maori lyrics and dance movements retain their essential character and conform to ritual conventions. Recent years have seen a steady return to true traditional songs and dances, and this has been stimulated by the South Pacific Festival of the Arts, in which all the ethnic groups of that area now regularly participate.

The quickening of interest in all things Maori owes much to the keen enjoyment most Pakeha derive from these colourful performances, which have so long been a feature on all important national occasions.

MAORI COSTUME ADDS COLOUR TO CEREMONIES

Everyday dress for the Maori today is no different from that of all New Zealanders, but on official observances he may well introduce to his apparel some item of traditional significance. An elder may wear a fine feather cloak which has been treasured by his family for generations, or hold a carved stick of historic significance to his tribe when welcoming visitors from another tribal area. The purpose of the cloak worn over everyday clothes may be to denote rank or status, or simply to bring into the assembly an appropriate Maori insignia. But even at purely Maori gatherings full old-time costume is no longer worn – it has been replaced by ordinary clothes – only Maori concert parties now dress up.

Some members of the party may possess prized heirlooms in the shape of woven and embroidered *kahu* (cloaks). Such a cloak is sometimes presented to a very distinguished visitor as a token of respect and esteem. It is fortunate that students today may still learn from the few older Maori women whose expert skills in the weaving of this, the most prestigious item of Maori costume, are being passed down to the present generation.

Bird feathers were the usual covering for a ceremonial cloak, each one being firmly linked into the finely woven base. Sometimes feathers covered the cloak completely, and where only one variety was used the cloak was called after the bird, e.g. *kahu kiwi* (a cloak of kiwi feathers). Some of the most beautiful of the old-time cloaks were patterned with the bright plumage of the more gaily coloured birds – the *kererū* (bush pigeon), and the *kakāriki* (parakeet), among many others. The hair of the native *kuri* (dog), now extinct, was also used in ancient times. Some splendid examples of early Maori clothing may be studied in the Maori sections of our principal museums.

The basic material for all items of clothing was obtained from the several varieties of the flax plant whose leaves yield a good, strong fibre. This was prepared by the women who stripped away the green cuticle, and carefully scraped and pounded the remaining fibre to a degree of fineness suited to the importance of the garment for which it would form the woven base.

But not all garments were actually woven. The distinctive Maori *piupiu* (kilt), worn by both sexes, and which adds such a unique sound to the dance as its wearers move, is of more simple, but no less skilled manufacture. Here the flax leaves are carefully separated into wide, even strands and the strand cleared of cuticle at precise intervals along its length, is dried. In drying, the strands roll into quill-like cylinders. The ends are plaited together until sufficient length is attained to make a waistband. The *piupiu* is then immersed in black mud which dyes the exposed fibres black but the quills retain the rich yellow colour of the dried leaf. Later the waistband may be attached to a woven border of patterned *tāniko* (ornamental border).

This same *tāniko* design is often repeated on the headband, *(tipare)*, womans' bodice *(pari)*, and on the edges of the cloak, the whole giving a uniform effect to the dress of a Maori Concert party. Over the past decade Maori scholars have published important books describing in detail the designing and making of traditional Maori clothing, and it is not surprising that the decorative patterns have spread into many other fields. Maori motifs are now frequently used in embroidery, knitting and in woven and dyed cloth sold as distinctive New Zealand commodities.

Rangihaeata, a famous Maori warrior chief, in full ceremonial dress. This portrait was painted in 1864 by C. D. Barraud. Note the greenstone mere (hand weapon), the hei tiki (human form neck pendant), and the richly decorated cloaks. All these were badges of rank and authority.

In a re-enactment of by-gone days, this group wearing full costume and personal ornaments, pose in front of the carved house "Mata-atua", in the Otago Museum, Dunedin.

PRESTIGIOUS ORNAMENTS

Stone, bone, and feathers were among the materials most favoured by the old-time Maori for fashioning into personal ornaments. Best known today of these ornaments is undoubtedly the *hei tiki* (neck pendant), usually made of "greenstone", more properly called nephrite and often referred to as New Zealand jade. This grotesquely shaped human-like figure has great *mana*. Especially is this the case when the tiki has been handed down through several generations of high ranking people. The fashioning of it may have taken a Maori craftsman several years, for nephrite is hard, (a little harder than window glass in fact), and the tools used to shape and polish it were themselves of stone. Nephrite must be ground, it cannot be roughly shaped by knapping as is the case with most stone.

Both men and women wore personal ornaments, but the *hei tiki* was and is, most frequently seen worn by a woman of rank. It takes the name *tiki* from the male spirit, implanted according to legend during creation, by Tane the god of nature, into the earth-formed maid.

Small wonder that these *tiki* are valued beyond price, and that the few women of today who hold them in trust, seldom if ever, take them off. Small wonder too, that some of the commerically produced Maori-type artifacts of this sort, are viewed with such distaste by those who recognise the significance of the originals. It is no disgrace to copy, but to copy badly is to discount historical concepts. Steps have recently been taken to authenticate items for the souvenir market, only when the article has the merit of reasonable accuracy.

The Maori name for greenstone is *pounamu*. This prized stone is found only in the South Island, which they named for it, *Te Wahi Pounamu* – the place of greenstone. There are a number of varieties, all of them valued, and all named with poetic allusion, e.g.

Inanga – The whitebait; this has a pearly whitish-green colour like the young of the river minnow.

Kawakawa – A rich dark green variety, similar in colour to the leaves of the kawakawa tree.

Tangiwai – Tear drops; this is a translucent sort having a tear drop like pattern throughout.

A highly prized personal ornament; a greenstone hei tiki.

TATTOO – A VERY PERSONAL ADORNMENT

The face of a tattooed Maori chief has always been a unique design feature on New Zealand currency, postage stamps and national and civic coats of arms. This form of personal adornment, once so distinctive a Maori usage, is now not often seen. It is said that the last tattooing was done prior to the visit of the then Prince of Wales in 1920, when some of the women selected for the official welcome ceremony had their lips and chins decorated with the traditional women's *moko* (tattoo). A few of these ladies still survive. However, recently Mrs Tawai Hauraki-Te Rangi, who teaches Maori at Heretaunga College, fulfilled the prophecy made by her grandfather, and had the *moko* pattern tattooed on her chin; since then two more Maori ladies and one man have followed her lead.

It was only the male who had his whole visage tattooed and in many cases the designs covered the body from knees to waist. Strangely, Tasman makes no mention of *moko,* though he describes the Maoris he saw. Cook however, has many references to the custom and this is an extract from his journal.

"The marks in general are spirals drawn with great nicity and even elegance. One side corresponds with the other. The marks on the body resemble foliage in old chased ornaments, convolutions of filigree work, but in these they have such a luxury of form that of a hundred which at first appeared exactly the same no two were formed alike on close examination".

The process carried on progressively from early manhood, must have been painful in the extreme. The *tohunga tā moko* (a priest skilled in the art) who was himself exempt from the practice, was an important personage. He was one of the principal exponents and supervisors of tribal lore and ritual, and the *moko* rite was of great personal and tribal significance. The pre-determined pattern was traced onto the skin, then following the lines a tiny bone chisel was repeatedly driven deep into the flesh. Before each incision the blade was dipped into a mixture of soot made from burnt kauri gum, or from burnt vegetable caterpillars. After these stoically endured wounds healed, an incised blue-stained scar remained as a permanent pattern. To ensure that his *moko* was never hidden, the old-time Maori plucked out his beard, hair by hair. Chiefs later used their personal *moko* designs as their signatures. Many examples of this use can be seen on the Treaty of Waitangi, now in the Alexander Turnbull Library, Wellington.

While the last of the tattooed Maori chieftains were still living, noted artists painted their portraits. Some of these portraits can be seen in New Zealand's principal art galleries. The most notable collection is in the Auckland City Art Gallery where Gottfried Lindauer's lifelike and wonderfully detailed work records the tattooed faces.

The tattooed heads of enemies, preserved by steaming, smoking and then drying were kept by the tribes as objects of contempt. Some of these heads were obtained by Europeans when the first sailing ships began to call, and soon a grisly trade sprang up which resulted in an extension of tribal warfare and many cases of cruel and unnecessary killings. Examples of these dried tattooed heads may be seen in our museums, and a study of them will show how the *moko* patterns were carried through to Maori wood sculptures.

An impressive portrait of a tattooed chief. Tomika Te Mutu is one of the many Maori leaders whose portraits were painted at the turn of the century, by Gottfried Lindauer. Auckland City Art Gallery holds an important collection of such paintings.

THE WOODCARVER AND HIS ART

Whakairo-rākau (wood sculpture), popularly called Maori carving, is well-known to all New Zealanders. The vigorous and wonderfully wrought art-form is an ongoing achievement of the race, and in the last half-century more important works have been produced than in any previous period of history. These vary from items as large as the 15m high *pouihi* (section carved pole), designed and carved by that great New Zealander, the late Inia Te Wiata, and erected in the foyer of New Zealand House in London, to the small exquisitely patterned *papahau* (treasure boxes), the traditional welcome gifts presented to visiting Royalty. Inia Te Wiata's immense *pouihi* symbolises the unity of both races and the continuity of the Maori past into the present and the future.

In the past the carver was of priestly rank, a *tohunga-waihanga*. His art was regarded with awe and the performance of it attended by rigid disciplines. Even today when the craftsman carver wearing a modern overall and using steel tools, goes to work, the rituals of the past are not entirely forgotten. This is as it should be, for his work draws inspiration from his history, legends, ancestors and heroes.

The bulk of Maori wood-sculpture being done now finds its way into the carved houses which have been, and are being erected throughout the country. As an extension of their earlier usage some urban maraes serve as community centres and are also seminar or conference halls for groups concerned with the well-being of the land and its people. Restoration too of existing houses is another task of today's carver.

Totara is the favoured timber for carving, and completed work was in the past coated with a mixture of red ochreous clay mixed with shark oil as a preservative. Small pieces like *wakahuia* (feather boxes), used for storing personal treasures were often left uncoated and over the years the wood took on a pleasing patina through constant handling.

The old stone-tooled carving has a softer look than that done with steel chisels, and well weathered examples of work of this early era are worth especial study. Fortunately most of our museums possess examples.

Today most Maori carvers are trained at Rotorua at the School of Maori Arts and Crafts, which fosters the ancient skills, and maintains traditional standards.

Strict rules have always been associated with the carver and his work. No food was eaten or even taken close to the workplace. Women should never approach it. The carver would not smoke while working, nor blow the chips away from his chisel or let them accumulate, but would bury them lest they should be used on a cooking fire. Dire misfortune is considered inevitable should these *tapu* rituals be violated, and there are well authenticated stories of death resulting after such offences.

Where these or any other carving rituals had been breached, the *tohunga* was consulted and after consideration of the gravity of the offence, he performed the appropriate ceremony of propitiation, and so allowed the project to proceed. Work not so cleared was abandoned and the carvings themselves considered to be malevolent and certain to bring ill fortune to anyone who should attempt to recover them.

Two distinct carving styles. On the left a pou tokomanawa *(middle support pole), in the carved house at Waitangi. It is a portrait in wood of a tattooed ancestor. On the right a stockade image from Rotorua; these were erected in the protective palisades surrounding a* pā *(fortified village), to glare defiantly at any attacker.*

Tourists strolling along the lakeside at Taupo pass through this carved gateway – a reminder of the historic Maori origins of the town and area.

RIGHT *The marae at Manukorihi Pa at Waitara, with the notable Taranaki carved house "Te Ikaroa-a-Maui (the long fish of Maui), seen through the carved gateway.*

The traditional carving rites have under modern conditions been loosened, but the tie still remains and observance is not entirely given up.

Master carvers of the present era, notably John and the late Pine Taiapa of the East Coast, Henare Toka of Northland and the late Piri Poutapu of Waikato have made this ancient art their lifetime occupation. Though most contemporary work is commissioned for use in tribal meeting houses, it is also seen today in many other appropriate situations. Churches, chapels, civic buildings, school assembly halls and even some boardrooms of this country's commercial enterprises, display with pride and sincerity appropriate examples of this distinctively New Zealand art.

Unhappily though, Maori "carvings" moulded in plastic have recently become all too common examples of New Zealand kitsch, for often the designs, and the uses to which they are put, are ludicrous.

The marae, with its ceremonial carved house will always be the most fitting setting for Maori artistry and craftsmanship. New Zealand and its visitors are fortunate to be able to see fine meeting houses throughout the length and breadth of the country. Not all of these are always open for public visits, but some, for example the house 'Tame-te-Kapua' at Ohinemutu, Rotorua, have become attractions of prime importance to tourists and to students. It is a veritable encyclopaedia of arts of the Maori.

ABOVE: A scene at the dedication ceremony of "Rongomai", the new urban marae which was opened at Upper Hutt on 22 August 1976. This is the fifth such centre built by Maori effort in the greater Wellington urban area, and there are many more such modern maraes throughout New Zealand.

"Tama-te-Kapua" at Ohinemutu is one of the best-known and most important carved houses. These photographs show the exterior, and a poupou *(interior carved panel).*

"TAMA-TE-KAPUA" – A MAORI MEETING HOUSE

The *whare-runanga* (meeting house), is not a modern concept. Though most recently built houses do incorporate innovations in the shape of additional features for the comfort and convenience of the people, the structural symbolism is always retained. This is based on the belief that the house is a material representation of a revered tribal ancestor. "Tame-te-Kapua" is a splendid example of this.

It was erected in 1878 and is named for the primal canoe ancestor of the Arawa people. In Maori symbolism the great ridge-pole supporting the roof is his backbone, the front main pole which holds up the ridge-pole is his heart, the rafters are his ribs, the window his eye, the door his mouth, the frontal facing boards his arms and the carved gable mask his head. Inside the house the interior panel carvings portray Arawa ancestors, and here we may see the legendary Tutanekai, his flute to his lips as his playing guides his beautiful lover, Hinemoa, who swam across Lake Rotorua to reach him on the island of Mokoia. On stilts is Tama-te-Kapua himself, who used this ruse to avoid footprints when raiding the sacred breadfruit tree of the high priest Uenuku, in the homeland of Hawaiki. Despite this precaution, he and his brother were caught in the act; war resulted. Tama-te-Kapua and Whakaturia were defeated and as a result built the canoe Te Arawa in which they and their followers reached New Zealand. So the Arawa tribe had its origins.

Many other tribal ancestors and heroes are featured on the *poupou* (carved interior panels). Between them are beautiful examples of *tukutuku* (lattice work) panels, their geometrical designs made by lacing black painted laths and *toetoe* (pampas grass) reeds, with flax and other fibrous leaves. The patterns themselves are meaningful, not merely random decoration.

The great curved rafters are painted in red, black and white patterns, repeated in rhythmic curves and spirals. The designs are traditional, their origins in some cases lost in the mists of antiquity. All, however, are based on the rhythms of nature, among them being the waves of the sea, the unfolding of the fern frond, and the symmetry of fishes. The designs are called *kowhai-whai*, from the *kokowai* (red clay), which formed the pigment for the paint used not only on the rafter patterns, but on most carvings. This red was to the old-time Maori the most beautiful of colours. Its replacement by garish modern enamels is deplored. The sombre yet rich matte red of the *kokowai*, preserves and enhances.

Early visitors to this country, from Captain Cook onwards, have given written descriptions of early Maori meeting houses, and artists, notably George French Angas who came to New Zealand before the event of photography, made detailed paintings of some important houses which have long since disappeared. In recent years many new houses have been built, especially in and around the larger cities, where about seventy per cent of the Maori people of today live and work. No longer do they dwell in tribal communities, in the classic village with its fortified *pa*. However, the marae and meeting house as the centre of cultural activity has not been allowed to become obsolete, but has taken on a broader aspect and now embraces the community as a whole.

Motupoi Pa on the shores of Lake Roto-Aira as it was in the 1840s when George French Angas visited New Zealand. He painted many scenes of Maori life and portraits of Maori people.

LIVING IN THE PAST

The old-time *pā* (fortified tribal villages), built as they were of wood and reeds, have long since disappeared, but oral tradition and written records, paintings and drawings made in the late 1700s early 1800s, give careful descriptions of them. Archaelogists too, working on the old sites, are able in certain cases to reconstruct the layout and establish the general appearance of local settlements. At the same time artifacts made of stone, shell, or bone which have withstood the ravages of time are often recovered. Sad to relate many old *pā* sites have in the past been heedlessly destroyed, some have been disturbed by curio hunters, and only now are effective steps being taken to preserve them for scientific examination.

There are many places where the trenches and ramparts, laboriously built so long ago, are still plainly visible. One Tree Hill overlooking Auckland City is a well known example. The fortified section of a *pā* was strategically sited on high ground. Inter-tribal raids and skirmishes occurred frequently, and the people of the village moved up behind the palisades when danger threatened. The watchtower which can be seen on the skyline in the painting by Marcus King, was always manned. From this tower too, and others in the defences, stones and darts were hurled at the approaching attackers, and even when no enemy was seen the sentry beat a suspended wooden gong to let the tribe know that he was alert, and perhaps to warn any lurking unfriendly scout that surprise attack was impossible.

In the painting we see the *pātaka* (storehouse) raised up on poles to keep out the native rat *(kiore)*. Like the meeting house, a *pātaka* was sometimes elaborately carved and in it precious tribal ornaments were kept. Plainer *pātaka* were used for storing preserved food. The man on the ladder-pole is rethatching the roof with the dried leaves of the *raupo* (bulrush).

In the foreground women are plaiting green flax leaves. These will serve as covers for cooking food in the *hāngi,* (ground oven) which was made by heating stones and putting these into a pit. The food was then placed on mats and covered with more mats, more hot stones, then with earth – an efficient process, and one still practised today at tribal gatherings. Green flax was also made into baskets for carrying and serving food. These are called *kono.*

An elderly woman weaving is seen on the right of the painting. She would be of high rank, for the making of ceremonial garments was not entrusted to commoners. This intricate process is carried out by the fingers only. No loom or shuttle is used, and like carving the operation is highly *tapu.* On the left a chief or *rangatira* (one of noble birth), wears a feather cloak around his shoulders, and the tail feathers of the huia in his hair. The feathers of the huia – a bird now extinct – were reserved for *ariki* (chiefs, priests, or the firstborn of noble families). In the distance a group of children play hand games. The Maori had many such games, all designed to foster mental alertness and manual dexterity.

At Whakarewarewa, Rotorua, "Rotowhio Pa" has been reconstructed as a tourist attraction. There is a similar reconstruction at Kerekeri, Northland.

This imaginative painting by Marcus King shows life in a Maori pa as it was in pre-European days.

The great carved war canoe "Te-Toki-a-Tapiri", and the carved storehouse "Te Oha", in the Maori Hall at the Auckland Institute and Museum.

UIA MAI, TOIA MAI, TE WAKA – BEHOLD THE CANOE

The title of this chapter is that of a popular action song, one of many songs and chants, some of which record the names of the canoes Arawa, Tainui, Tokomaru, Aotea, Mataatua, Kurahaupo and Takitimu which between the tenth and twelfth centuries carried the Maori colonists across the Pacific Ocean from Polynesia to their new home. It is from these canoes that the Maori tribes trace their origins, and such songs keep alive the names of the notable personages who made the journey, and often refer to incidents which happened during that great adventure.

As his legends and history show, the old-time Maori was a bold and skilful seaman. After he settled in his new land which he called *Te Ika a Maui* (the fish caught by Maui) – Maui is the demi-god who is credited with the raising of the North Island out of the ocean – canoes laboriously fashioned by fire and by stone tools, from the great trunks of the magnificent trees now available to him, sailed on all the waterways. It was the sea which provided a great deal of his diet. From the rivers and lakes too, he got protein foods. It was the canoe which carried him on journeys of exploration expeditions of war, and visits of friendship. Small wonder that its builders were so highly regarded and that their craft reached such a peak of perfection.

A lively account of the war canoe and its crew is given by R. A. Cruise, writing in 1820, at the Bay of Islands:

"The largest we saw was 84 feet long, 6 feet wide and 5 deep . . . It was made of a single cowry-tree, hollowed out . . . impelled by the united force of ninety naked men . . . three others standing upon the thwarts regulated the strokes of the paddles, by repeating with violent gestures, a song in which they were joined by every one in the vessel. The canoe moved with astonishing rapidity, causing the water to foam on either side of it."

Records show that after the signing of the Treaty of Waitangi, a flotilla of no less than sixty-nine canoes left on a single day for Hawke's Bay carrying the members of a returning tribe back to their homes. As late as the 1860s, sea battles involving canoe fleets were still being fought by warring tribes and during the land wars, British troops operating along the Waikato River made frequent use of war canoes. One of these, "Teremoe", now displayed in the National Museum in Wellington is an impressive example of canoe construction. It was on these great war canoes that the Maori lavished his most expert workmanship, both as a marine architect and as an artist.

One is fortunate indeed to be a guest at Waitangi or at Ngaruawahia when the splendid carved war canoes, housed at both these maraes, are launched with traditional ceremony, to mark some historic event.

One of the three war canoes from the Tūrangawaewae marae, on the Waikato River near Ngaruawahia. These canoes are launched with appropriate ceremony, on historic occasions.

ABOVE AND RIGHT: Cooking in the hāngi *(earth oven). Heating the stones. The stones and covered food are carefully put into the pit. A covering of earth is added. The food now cooked is served.*

FOOD YESTERDAY AND TODAY

Fishing canoes were not so lavishly decorated as war canoes, yet the few prows of old fishing canoes which still survive are of special interest to students of Maori art. The carving is more austere; the carvers seem to have worked outside convention and achieved a realism absent from more formal projects. This is also sometimes evident in the decoration of articles made for domestic use, particularly those employed in the gathering and storage of food.

The old-time tribesmen were, as many early writers report, good trenchermen in times of plenty. *Hākarai* (great feasts) at which enormous quantities of food were consumed, were and still are a popular way of celebrating an important event. But food was not always plentiful, nor was it easily got, and usually only two meals were eaten, one mid-morning, and one at sunset. These were always consumed outdoors, for food was never taken inside a house.

Until the coming of the white settlers there were no large food animals. Human flesh often filled this want, for the victors feasted on the bodies of the vanquished, and wars were frequent. All males were trained from boyhood in the martial arts, and though in a crisis women sometimes fought alongside their warrior tribesmen, it is said that they were not allowed the customary *kai tangata* (man food) which followed a successful battle.

A great deal of food came from the sea, for the Maori was an expert fisherman with both net and line. The stranding of a whale or other large sea creature was a bonus which occasioned great rejoicing, for food gathering on land or from the sea was a task without end.

Of the native vegetable foodstuffs fernroot was generally the most important. It was available in all seasons but the most palatable roots were deep in the ground and no more than finger thick. Much heavy work was needed to dig enough to feed a hungry *whānau* (family group), and only after pounding with a heavy *patu* (mallet), to separate out the stringy fibres, was it made into an acceptable repast. The sow-thistle or *pūwhā* was and still is a popular green. Even today Maori families may be seen gathering this common plant which seems to flourish by the roadsides. Berries; karaka, tawa, hinau and tutu among others, were all collected in their seasons, and from the crushed kernels of the hinau a kind of bread was made. The heavy yellow pollen of the raupo was laboriously harvested and this too, was made into a sort of loaf.

From Polynesia the Maori introduced four crop plants. Where he was successful in establishing these, but in particular the *kūmara,* (sweet potato), agriculture soon flourished and so did the tribes which practised it.

Propitiation of the appropriate god was rigidly observed when gathering food. Tane, for the food from the forest, Tangaroa, for the food from the sea, Rongo, for the fruits of agriculture. The *atua* (god spirit), was believed to dwell not only in the places where food was got, but also in some of the implements used in its cultivation or capture. Small wonder that the ancient Maori was a natural conservationist!

After the establishment of European settlement, diet quickly changed. Cannibalism was soon dropped. Meat, especially pork, became plentiful and was

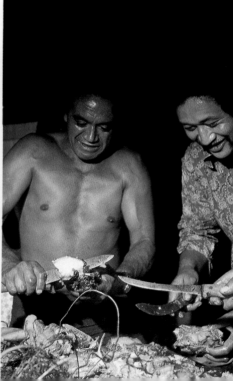

relished. The potato, less demanding in soil requirements and producing a heavier crop, almost completely replaced the kumara. Traditional Maori foods were used less and less; soon the Englishman's "bread, beef, beer and cheese" largely replaced them.

Today, the Maori is still reckoned to be a good trencherman. His capacity for food is matched by his lavish hospitality, as anyone who has been fortunate to have been a guest at a *hui* (ceremonial gathering), will attest. From the *hāngi* (earth oven), comes steaming mountains of food, an appetising assortment of the modern and the traditional, and the *kai moana* (sea foods) of his forefathers are still relished and indeed preferred, be they served at a hui, in the home or at a restaurant.

Maoris are rightly resentful of the fact that our coastal waters are being depleted of such delicacies as *kōura* (crayfish), *kina* (sea eggs), *pāua* (a large shellfish), by commercial interests fishing for the world's wealthy gourmet markets, and by greedy poachers who ignoring size and season clean out the beds giving no opportunity for restocking. Sadly, the old-time gods no longer take a hand to avenge such wrongs. In the days of ancient legends, Tangaroa, the god of the sea, would summon his forces. From huge *tōhora* (the whale), to tiny *inanga* (the whitebait), they would gather as an avenging army to destroy such violators of the ocean kingdom.

A hui (ceremonial gathering) at Manahanea marae at Ruatoria. This is a tribal centre for the Ngati Porou people. At gatherings such as this ties of kinship and aroha (love and affection) are renewed and strengthened. The carved meeting house, "Hinepora" dates from 1896, but contains a number of carvings of an earlier era.

Commemorating a legendary incident is this statue of the Maori heroine Wairaka on a rock on the foreshore at Whakatane. In the twelfth century she defied custom and successfully acting the part of a man, saved the Mataatua canoe from becoming wrecked. An ancient story with a modern sentiment!

FABLES AND FACTS

Told by the elders, recorded and published by the scholars, the legends and fables of the Maori people, today form one of the most significant sections of our literature. Indeed they are the only true indigenous stories the nation can claim, for the Pakeha is a relative newcomer, his origins are cosmopolitan and it is to the Maori the writer must turn for authentic New Zealand strength and substance. He is fortunate that there is such a wealth of material, and fortunate too that Maoritanga continues to flourish though it has moved from the fabled past into the material present.

The new generation Maori, now-a-days mainly a city dweller, has while still strongly influenced by the oral literature of his forefathers, added to it the art of written expression. He encompasses in his work the echoes of yesterday and today's more strident sounds. Respect for his past and concern for the future of the land and the people, are frequent themes. This is to be expected for young adults now make up the greatest proportion of the Maori population, over two-thirds being under 25 years of age.

The studied discontent manifested world-wide by the youth of today, has found expression in Maori youth too – and perhaps with good reason. We now see issues raised and debated by the young which were once the prerogative of the elders. Group action unrelated to any tribal ties finds support from Maoris affiliated to church, political, social, educational and sporting organisations. But seldom are such groups purely Maori, even the few that claim to be so have a sprinkling of Pakeha supporters. So through respect, understanding and common interests the races merge. Slowly a distinctive New Zealand culture is emerging; the remaining areas of Maori discontent, being shared, begin to be rectified. There is still much to be done, and much that will be done as long as all New Zealanders remember with pride: *He iwi tāhi tātou* – We are one people.

Young generation New Zealanders. They will become the custodians of the nation's culture, and inherit from both races the blend which has bred the distinctive character of the "Kiwi".

AUTHOR'S NOTE AND BIBLIOGRAPHY

I should like to record my thanks to the Department of Maori affairs, and in particular to Joy Stevenson, Sam Ruawai and Witi Ihimaera for help with the text, and to the photographers named in the credits.

If this little book could be regarded as were the chips from the carver's chisel, or the scraps of fibre left over from the weaving of a cloak, I should be happy. These were small unimportant fragments in themselves, but they were used to fertilise the soil which has grown the trees and the flax from whence they came. So, I hope interest will be stimulated in the bigger and more scholarly books on Maori life and culture, which I have consulted. Among them are:

Armstrong A. and Ngata R., Maori Action Songs: Wellington 1960.
Barrow T. T., The Life and Work of the Maori Carver: Wellington 1963.
Barrow T. T., The Decorative Arts of the N.Z. Maori: Wellington 1964.
Buchanan, J. D. H., The Maori History and Place Names of Hawke's Bay: 197
Dansey H. D. B., How the Maoris Came to Aotearoa: Wellington 1975.
Ihimaera W., Maori: Wellington 1975.
Mead S. M., Traditional Maori Clothing: Wellington 1969.
Phillipps W. J., Maori Life and Custom: Wellington 1966.
Reed A. W., Myths and Legends of Maoriland: Wellington 1961.
Reed A. W., Concise Maori Dictionary: Wellington 1971.
Salmond Anne, Hui – A study of Maori Ceremonial: Wellington 1975.
Stafford D. M., Te Arawa: Wellington 1967.
Yate William, An Account of New Zealand: London 1835.